THE METHOD OF ZEN

By the same Author

ZEN IN THE ART OF ARCHERY

THE METHOD OF

ZEN

by

EUGEN HERRIGEL

Edited by

HERMANN TAUSEND

Translated from the German by

R. F. C. HULL

LONDON

ROUTLEDGE AND KEGAN PAUL

Translated from the German

DER ZEN WEG

First published in England 1960
by Routledge & Kegan Paul Ltd
Broadway House, Carter Lane
London, E.C.4

© *Otto Wilhelm Barth-Verlag 1958*

English translation
© *Routledge & Kegan Paul Ltd 1960*

Printed in Great Britain
by Latimer, Trend & Co. Ltd., Plymouth

Contents

Introductory

THE WAY TO ZEN BUDDHISM

SOON AFTER I arrived in Japan, a meeting took place with some Japanese colleagues in Tokyo. We were having tea together in a restaurant on the fifth floor of a hotel.

Suddenly a low rumbling was heard, and we felt a gentle heaving under our feet. The swaying and creaking, and the crash of objects, became more and more pronounced. Alarm and excitement mounted. The numerous guests, Europeans mostly, rushed out into the corridor to the stairs and lifts. An earthquake—and a terrible earthquake a few years before was still fresh in everyone's memory. I too had jumped up in order to get out into the open. I wanted to tell the colleague with whom I had been talking to hurry up, when I noticed to my astonishment that he was sitting there unmoved, hands folded, eyes nearly closed, as though none of it concerned him. Not like someone who hangs back irresolutely, or who has not made up his mind, but like someone who, without fuss, was doing something—or not doing something—perfectly naturally. The sight of him was so astounding and had such a sobering effect that I remained standing beside him, then sat down and stared at him fixedly, without even asking myself what it could mean and whether it was advisable to remain. I was spell-bound—I don't know by what—as though nothing could happen to me. When the earthquake was over—it was said to have lasted a fairly long time—he continued the conversation at the exact point where he had broken off, without wasting a single word on what had happened. For my part I was quite unable to pay attention, and probably gave stupid answers. With the terror still chilling my limbs, I asked myself rather: What prevented me from running away? Why did I not follow an instinctive impulse? I found no satisfactory answer.

A few days later I learned that this Japanese colleague was a Zen Buddhist, and I gathered that he must have put himself into a state of extreme concentration and thus become 'unassailable'.

Although I had read about Zen before, and heard a few things about it, I had only the vaguest idea of the subject. The hope of penetrating into Zen—which had made my decision to go to Japan very much easier—changed, as a result of this dramatic experience, into the intention to start without further delay. I was more concerned with the mysticism of Zen, with the way that led beyond the 'unassailability'. It was not my colleague's imperturbable behaviour—impressive as it was— that hovered before me as a goal, for there are other methods of attaining this without having to go to Japan.

In the meantime I was informed that it was not so easy to penetrate more deeply into Zen, because Zen had no theory and no dogma. I was advised to turn to one of the arts which were most strongly influenced by Zen, and thus to make contact with it by a slow and roundabout route. This advice I followed. In my book *Zen in the Art of Archery* I have given an account of this course of instruction.

ZEN AND THE CLASSIC METHODS OF MEDITATION

Buddhist mysticism differs from all other mysticism in the emphasis it lays on a methodical preparation for the mystical life. It has made meditation into an art, in which technique not only plays its rightful role, as in every art, but occupies an uncommonly large place. It has thus performed a service of quite incalculable merit: it has rescued

3

the practice of mysticism from the element of chance. It, too, describes the concentrated efforts that lead to self-immersion as a 'way', but nowhere else has the way, the method of meditation, acquired such fundamental importance.

The Far East owes an infinite amount to the way of the Buddha. It has produced a unique type of hieratic man. It is not for us to inquire whether the high level once reached has been preserved everywhere in Buddhism down to the present day; nor whether strict method has turned into routine, and enlightenment into esoteric knowledge.

Our concern is with Zen Buddhism. We shall not discuss when, how, and through whom it arose, but only why it was that Zen, although essentially a part of Buddhism, as regards its method took a different course from the classic Buddhist mystique of meditation.

It is a striking fact that, in Buddhism, enlightenment consists in a pure vision of the same truths with which the work of meditation begins. The insights that prompted the retreat from the world return again in abstract form, devoid of all admixture of emotion, thus sanctioning the original experience of the Buddha which started him on the way to enlightenment. Is not this result explained by the fact that the theme for meditation becomes, as it were, a fixed idea?

The Buddhist starts from the assumption that life is suffering. But what if the original experience were different: if life were felt to be enjoyable and the world a delightful harmony, would not en-lightenment be coloured accordingly? It would then be very difficult to understand why anybody should wish to detach himself from this delightful and harmonious world.

Obviously, no one meditating in any such way ever gets beyond himself. He does not get *beyond* thinking and not-thinking, pleasure and pain, etc., but merely reaches a zone of indifference, which he declares is a 'Beyond'. With what, then, is a *unio mystica* performed? All the meditant has done is to detach himself from what does not belong to his true being, finding, in consequence, even at the deepest level of his being, only himself.

Logically, therefore, it must be possible to prac-tise meditation and concentration without a set theme, to follow a way without holding on to any-thing solid and objective, with no philosophical assumptions of any kind, experiencing the world as neither full of sorrow nor full of joy, as meriting neither hate nor love, transient though it may be. A 'philosophy' should rather be the product of enlightenment. That enlightenment exists, the Buddha himself has promised. Perhaps it will turn out to be quite different from the Buddhist one if nothing is suggested into it. The way of the Buddha indicates that this must be possible. There is, in Buddhism, a stage of indifference when you stand at the neutral point between knowing and not-knowing, no longer directing your mind to anything. But—in Buddhist meditation you are cumbered by all the preceding stages.

What would happen if you meditated in an 'unpremeditated' way from the beginning? Simply practised sinking into yourself, becoming completely empty, with no programme, letting come what may?

That was the way of Zen. We cannot tell how far back 'Nothing' was sought in this fashion, but the existence of Zen in China and Japan shows that the search was successful. That it succeeded brilliantly is proved by the vitality of Zen up to the present. Only one thing remains difficult to understand: what reason would the Zen adept have for turning away from the world if his attitude to the world is, from a philosophical point of view, entirely neutral? A historical explanation could be given for this: he knew that there is enlightenment and a way to it. Afterward he could say that the experience he went through was the 'great liberation'. But from what? In what sense?

ZEN CONTRASTED WITH EUROPEAN MYSTICISM

In Zen, man does not have the central position he has in European mysticism, where the *unio mystica* appears as the overwhelmingly blissful privilege to which he, as a human being, is entitled. He alone, of all the living creatures, is destined for this experience, and by attaining it he steps out of the state of being-in-the-world. This stepping out he calls 'ecstasy' (*ek-stasis*); it is losing himself and finding himself again, dying and being born again. What he finds again is his true centre, his inalienable self, which is cancelled out and yet preserved in the *unio mystica*. In God, in the Godhead, or whatever else European mystics term that with which and in which the union is accomplished, the self is not finally extinguished, but is saved, reprieved, and its fate sealed forever. Only temporarily, only for the sake of the ultimate at-one-ment which tolerates no duality, is 'dying to self' demanded, because God is born only into those souls that have offered up 'being themselves' as the final and supreme sacrifice. But once the birth is accomplished, the soul becomes the divinely empowered centre from which to be itself forever, evolving out of itself like Nietzsche's ever-rolling wheel.

7

In Zen, on the other hand, human existence as such is 'ek-static' and 'ek-centric', whether we are aware of it or not. The more a human being feels himself a self, tries to intensify this self and reach a never attainable perfection, the more drastically he steps out of the centre of being, which is no longer now his own centre, and the further he removes himself from it.

For the Zen Buddhist everything that exists, apart from man—animals and plants, stones, earth, air, fire, water—lives undemandingly from the centre of being, without having left it or being able to leave it. If man, having strayed from this centre, is to know security and innocence of existence as they live it, because ultimately they live without purpose, there is no alternative for him but a radical reversal. He must go back along the way whose thousand fears and tribulations have shown it to be a way of error, must slough off everything that promised to bring him to himself, renounce the seductive magic of a life lived on his own resources, and return home to the 'house of truth' which he wantonly left in order to chase phantoms when he was scarcely fledged. He must not 'become as a little child', but like forest and rock, like flower and fruit, like wind and storm.

The *unio mystica* in Zen therefore means home-coming, restoration of an original state now lost.

And so, in order to live from the centre like animals and plants and everything else, man must go the way which negates everything in him that is off-centre.

In the Far East this reversal and homecoming are not left to chance. The way can be prepared and methodically followed, above all in Japan.

Against this Zen Buddhist interpretation of existence it might be objected that the Oriental has never in his long history, not even today, fallen so hopelessly away from nature as the European. This is undoubtedly true and can be confirmed by a glance at his daily life, and more particularly at his art. But it must be realized that even unbroken nearness to nature is a long way from nearness to Zen. Nature, however it be regarded intellectually, is far from being the all-embracing truth by which Zen seeks to live. Nor is anything gained by pointing out that the Oriental—and especially the Japanese—has not extricated himself from the ties of tradition despite the modernization of his life in the economic, political, and technological spheres. This objection misses the mark, because at the time when Zen Buddhism reached Japan there was no question of life being modernized. So although people in those days lived in unbroken nearness to nature, and under the sway of a tradition to which they gave unquestioning assent, it did not deter the

Zen Buddhist from regarding this security of existence as 'eccentric', as a falling away, and finally as a sin.

For the Zen Buddhist there is a falling away and a sin in the very possibility of living largely on one's own resources. Man feels and experiences himself as an ego. Egohood leads to selfishness and self-assertion in the face of everything that is not-self, and hence to hardness of heart. He feels himself and makes himself the centre, if not consciously, then in secret. This attitude tends to become more and more acute, but it need not even be carried to an extreme. For the Zen Buddhist the very first selfish impulses of a child are unavoidable and pernicious. Therefore it is no argument to say that the Oriental has never fallen away from nature like the European and still lives in the framework of tradition. This does not preclude a constant struggle with his egohood, with the result that he is very far from living out of himself as though he were being lived, and from being lived as though he were living out of himself.

The special danger is that the ordinary man is in such a state of unawareness that he does not know this, and even if he is told cannot understand. His egohood goes hand in hand with a distortion of reality. So disturbed is his vision that he cannot see the difference between what he is

and what he should be. For what he should be, and
how he can become it, cannot be put before him
as a guiding image. It is not a different way of
living, a new direction given to his everyday
existence, not an image which he could bring into
reality, nothing that could be achieved with consciousness and will, with serious purpose and a
sense of responsibility. It is something totally
different, something that eludes his will and reason
and can be achieved only by a radical transformation.

That is why Zen Buddhism does not preach.
Sermons remain words. It waits until people feel
stifled and insecure, driven by a secret longing.

ZEN AS IT APPEARS TO WESTERN EYES

Mysterious, unfathomable, and unutterable as the
mystic experience itself is, the road that leads to it
should not be. It is meant to be accessible to anyone
of good will, if only in stretches, as measured out
to him by fate. There is thus a practicalness about
Zen which inspires confidence. So it is not surprising if, for the same reason that the way has to
be divided up, schematically and thematically, into
single steps, the learning of these steps should turn
into a regular routine. There is a rigorous training

in Zen which strikes one as utterly soulless. Everything must go with clockwork precision.

It is distressing to the European—but not to the Oriental—that the teachers seem to pay no attention to the personal peculiarities of their pupils. They make no allowance for special forms of development and for the individually differentiated consequences of this development; they suppress them, hold them in contempt, cut everything to the same pattern.

In order to understand this, it is of little help to say: The East is impersonal. On the contrary, the Masters know very well that there are deep-seated differences in individuals, but they also know—and here again they differ from Europeans—precisely where in the realm of mysticism these differences may be permitted to make their appearance, where they may not only be tolerated but are actually justified. And this is certainly not on the road to mystical experience, for there it is essential to negate everything individual, to depotentiate it to the utmost, so that one is completely 'emptied' even of one's most personal qualities. For this reason it is in the highest degree questionable whether the peculiarities we are endowed with by nature do really possess any 'personal' value at all. All the twists and turns of character of which we are so proud are perhaps, at bottom, impersonal.

The teachers succeed in putting their pupils through this apparently soulless discipline thanks to their astounding psychological experience, for they themselves have travelled the same path; moreover, they have at their disposal the accumulated experience of centuries. Great Masters can do the most amazing things in this respect, sometimes bordering on the incredible. The pupil who doubts their capacity to see into every corner of his soul soon learns that his resistance, whether conscious or instinctive, is in vain. Naturally, the Oriental seldom finds himself in this position. Unstinting veneration of his teacher is in his blood; it is part of his tradition. For the Master gives him his best, which will also be the pupil's best—his best in a spiritual sense. This consists least of all in things of the intellect which can be detached from the original giver, leaving him forgotten, but in that wealth of spiritual power which only one who has experienced it possesses, and which—logically—is not his own.

If the pupil is ever to have mystical experiences he will owe them solely to his teacher. For him the fate of his pupil is as important as his own fate; he is ready to sacrifice himself in the performance of his duty. Above all—and this must be especially emphasized—he always has time for his pupils.

As a result, the relationship of pupil to master is

one of absolute confidence and unquestioning devotion. The Master, on his side, accepts this gratitude, veneration, and love as something not due to him personally, for his power does not derive from himself and from what, through his own efforts, he has made of himself, but from the *unio*. Consequently he sees in it no cause for self-satisfaction. But he does not forbid his pupil's devotion; he accepts it as inevitable so long as the pupil is dependent on his spiritual leadership and has not yet related himself to the centre. Once this centre is found, the relationship will no longer be one of faith and trust, but of knowledge.

Anything the Master asks will be done by the pupil—not with the ostentatious assiduity of the religious careerist (all such soon drop out of the school), but from an inner impulse of dedication. This can be seen from the way the pupils speak of the Master among themselves—with a kind of sacred awe. For them he is the model and prototype, and even their exceedingly sharp and discerning eyes can detect no fault in him, although they are constantly in his presence. The disaster, otherwise, would be total, for their whole world would collapse. And the Master, if he were conscious of even the smallest imperfection in himself, would voluntarily renounce his high office and cease to lead others. For on the long and self-

abnegating path of Zen there are so many ob-
stacles, disappointments, and failures that if the
pupils could not put blind trust in the Master, and
find this trust vindicated at all times, they would
not be able to stay the course. This faith alone sustains them; not the conviction that they will reach
the goal, but that the Master is leading them in the
right direction—so far as it is their destiny to go.
And should they have to break off before reaching
the goal, they know that it is worth a whole life to
have gone even that much of the way. What keeps
them going is not direct faith in ultimately reaching the goal, for that is far off and as yet without
effect. But it becomes effective through the Master; and thus faith in the Master is, indirectly, faith
in the goal.

The schematization of the way, the mechanizing
of instruction, the relation of pupil to teacher—
all this helps us to understand why, from the very
beginning, there were 'schools' of mysticism in the
Far East; and why neither the way nor the experience of truth nor the life of the initiate was left to
chance, but was subjected to systematic training
and influence. There have never been schools of
mysticism in this sense in the West, not even as
tentative experiments. A master mystic was expected to burst forth from the skies, flashing for a
short while like a meteor, then vanishing again.

Any records he left behind would be much read and admired for a time, and remain not without influence on a small and devoted community. But in the long run, all it had to hold on to was the original inspiration; everyone took from it what suited him, finally the community split up into factions over the interpretation of his words. The Western mystic may have kindled men's hearts, but they did not go on burning, because they were not set on a path that supplied fuel enough, from personal experience, for the flame never to be extinguished.

In what follows I shall try to describe the schooling and transformation of those who enter upon this path in Japan, in the Zen Buddhist monasteries.

But I must preface this with a more general remark. Anyone who has had the good fortune to spend a number of years in close association with Japanese Zen Buddhists cannot help observing even the most trivial details of their daily life, as though in this way it would be possible to solve the riddle they present. He becomes aware, almost with dismay, that he is consorting with a people of a quite different mould from the ordinary. They seem to be ruled by a special star, not only in what they do, in their talk, in their silences, but more particularly in their casual behaviour: in the way they stand or walk, or drink tea, or drive away a mosquito. It is as if the world they live in had set its own incomparable stamp on their whole being, so that nothing happens in them and around them that has not entered—or is beginning to enter—into palpable relationship with them, with the invisible centre that determines their fate and the quality of their existence. They themselves never speak of what it is that moves them inwardly (and does not move them), nor do they feel any urge to make confessions. With an impenetrable smile they withdraw from investigation and completely ignore all questions put by mere curiosity. Their secret can be approached only by one who is on the way to experiencing it himself.

TRAINING IN ZEN BUDDHIST MONASTERIES

As is customary in the Far East, the young pupils of a monastery who are destined for priesthood seldom go there of their own accord. Generally they are obeying the wish of their parents. But they make this wish so much their own that it might be their own impulse. Otherwise, they would find no satisfaction. For the career of a priest is not exactly inviting: a rigorous life full of privations, yet its poverty is compensated by such inner riches that they would not exchange it for any other. Apart from these pupils, there are others who come to practise in the meditation halls in Zen Buddhist monasteries; pupils of all grades who are preparing for a career or have already finished their training, among them artists of all kinds. These come for a temporary stay of their own accord, somehow attracted by the spirit of Zen, and believing that closer contact with it will give them something which they may not ignore, not only for the sake of their profession but for their own sakes.

These older pupils have already been moulded by the experience of life or by their profession, and have perhaps proved their ability. And that is of value for their selection and admission, for their being singled out by a Master. They already have a fairly wide range of duties, and they may also have gone through a stiff course of training the will and the intellect. Surprising as it may seem, this is considered important. For what they are to learn in the monastery—concentration in order to meditate—requires the capacity to concentrate on the same thing for hours, days, and weeks on end. This presupposes firmness and steadiness of will no less than a clear intellect. The predominantly emotional type of person finds this very hard; indeed, he may make no headway at all.

A helpful factor is that the Japanese has learned from childhood to submit to discipline. It is astonishing and, for the European, almost inconceivable how much time the Japanese spend in restraining and controlling gestures which can at most be regarded as aesthetic faults. Say someone slams the door in a temper. In the East this is not taken as a sign of character, the expression of a forceful personality, nor is it regarded as a lapse which should not be taken seriously. Anyone who does such a thing will not, like the European, deem it justified by the situation, or excuse himself by saying that his feelings ran away with him. He will go back to the door, open it, close it softly, and say to it: 'I beg your pardon.' Thereafter he will take care how he shuts doors. Or perhaps he has received a parcel. He tears it open impatiently and throws the string and paper away. Too late he remembers that he has lost face by his impatience and curiosity. In future he will compose himself, carefully undo the string and wrapping, and put them aside, and only then examine the contents. Or again, he is expecting an important letter. It arrives. How easy it is to yield to the impulse to tear it open and hastily scan it. So he condemns himself to laying the letter aside and turning to something else until he has conquered his haste, and the letter is forgotten. When he sets his hand to it later, he opens it as though the envelope were something precious.

A European will think: They have time. No,

they do not have time, they take time. Or he will say: 'How fussy they are!' No, they want to become unfussy. He will ask: 'What does it all lead to?' To this: that those who are patient in small and trivial things, and control themselves, will one day have the same mastery in great and important matters. Great value, therefore, is set on moral character and observance of the social and ethical order, not as the final goal—Zen gets beyond that standpoint—but as an initial stage.

This training of will and intellect is complemented and supported by a spare, simple diet, physical work for recreation, with no more than the necessary amount of sleep on a hard bed. Discipline is exceedingly strict. Punctuality, conscientiousness, self-control are demanded, and ability to withstand heat and cold regardless of the weather.

From this point of view the influence of Zen Buddhism on the samurai is understandable; in fact, the samurai 'spirit' was largely moulded by it. Even today the instruction in archery and swordsmanship is distinguished by its strict discipline. The early hours of morning are chosen for practice, when one is clear-headed. The change in the seasons makes no difference; the coldest and the hottest times of the day are preferred.

The training of the younger pupils is different:

they are in every respect beginners, unwritten pages. The Master must first get to know them before he can put them on the Zen way. Hence, to begin with, their activities are quite different from what might be expected. They have to clean rooms, work in the kitchen, in the fields and garden. All the time they are covertly watched by the instructor. Not only speed, skill, and taste count, even more important are willingness, zeal, conscientiousness, unselfishness, readiness to serve. They go through a kind of testing time, with the undeceivable eye of the Master upon them. Least of all he watches how they behave toward him. It goes without saying that they treat him with reverence, but this is not revealing enough. And how they behave with their fellow pupils, what they talk about, is not characteristic enough. For even in a monastery the general style and atmosphere are something they can adapt to—they can always 'act up'. Therefore, to pay attention to what someone does *not* do is often more important than noting what he does. On the other hand, the handling of things, tools, etc., especially when the pupil thinks he is unobserved, tells the Master a great deal. He has reduced this to a fine art, and can probably read more out of it than a graphologist can from a person's handwriting. With his pupils he is uncompromising, strict, brusque, their antagonist in the truest sense of the word. But it is the severity of goodness, unswayed by moods and emotions. In the history of Zen Buddhism there are many examples of a Master's pitiless severity, but the pupil cannot yet see, as he will later, that everything was done out of compassion.

Once the pupil has reached a certain point, the real instruction—which may with reservation be called 'spiritual'—begins. The specifically spiritual training starts with *purification of the power of vision.* First one is required to perceive everything that is present, in all its sensuous fullness, including everything that is displeasing or repellent, and to hold it permanently in the mind. Again and again you have to immerse yourself in the contents of perception, until you know them by heart and can, at will, call them to mind in such a way that they present themselves without loss of clarity.

When you can do this, you must learn to rise above it, to apprehend what you are looking at as if from the inside, to look through it and grasp its essence, just as the painter does with a few concentrated strokes. From this we can see how much art owes to Zen.

Then, when that has been fully mastered, an intensification can be aimed at: holding the landscape, the fields with trees, flowers, cattle, and people, so intently in your gaze that in spite of the wood you still see the trees, and then thinning out the reality of the detail until you can grasp the unchanging character of the whole and retain it in its most concentrated form. Finally, even this vision of pure essence must be transcended; you must be able to picture the world itself, the cosmos, and—ultimately—infinite space, thereby expanding the power of vision still further. It is possible that everything will drift off into vagueness at this point, but even so, these exercises are not without effect.

Practising the power of vision does not lead only to increased capacity for concentration as such. Those with mystical experience who have tasks to perform in real life also need this enhanced power of vision, as we shall see.

Only when this stage has been reached does the real work of meditation begin.

BREATHING EXERCISES

The instruction which can with reservation be called 'spiritual' is concerned with breathing exercises in the Lotus position. It is easy for a Japanese to learn this position, because from a child he sits cross-legged on the floor, on a cushion, and learns to sit in a chair, or on a bench, only when he goes to school. For a European this way of sitting is painful at first and therefore disturbing because his attention should not be distracted. To begin with, he will have to be content to sit with legs half-crossed, or on a chair. But those who can manage the Lotus position without strain will agree that it induces a feeling of absolute privacy. So much depends on the position being comfortable, because the breathing is meant to induce complete relaxation of the body. This is done by concentrating on the act of breathing itself. You breathe in and out in a natural rhythm, but each breath is drawn consciously; at first it is even counted. Breathe out with emphasis, as it has a detaching effect. The better you can do this, the more immune you become to external impressions. In the end they are hardly registered at all. Relaxation occurs simultaneously. Finally you are nothing but breathing—you are breathed. Your breathing, left to itself and no longer consciously noticed, has found its own rhythm. It reduces itself to a minimum, which is just enough. (At this point there is some danger of dozing off, but in the monasteries this is guarded against by giving the pupil a smart blow on the back with a long stick.)

This is also the point when, the more vigorously the world outside is shut out, the world inside wakes up. After the elimination of external stimuli, this is the source of experience which the instructor has to block. You must not be astonished at anything that comes up, no matter how shameful. Accept it all calmly, as if you were a mere spectator, uninterested, and were observing a process for which you need not feel responsible. Simply let it go on until it wearies of itself, while you listen with only half an ear. The result, in the end, is perfect stillness, which breathes without your noticing it.

This stillness vanishes completely as soon as your attention is summoned awake and directed to something new. With this summons, a series of exercises begins in which concentration is combined with meditation. These exercises take place in the meditation hall or in a special room, which is not too light and must be cool and quiet, in an atmosphere of the deepest calm. Now and then they are interrupted by pauses, in which you walk around in the garden, but still immersed in the problem.

THE KOAN

The subject for meditation is the koan. It requires a supreme mental effort and permits of no lazy daydreaming. Here are a few examples of koans:

Show me your original face before you were born.

If you meet someone in the street who has attained to the truth, you must pass him neither speaking nor in silence. How would you meet him?

The priest Shusan held his staff[1] before the eyes of the assembled monks and said: 'If you call this a stick, it is disgusting. If you don't call it a stick, it is wrong. What will you call it?'

Hakuin[2] held his hand up in the air and told his pupils to listen to the sound it made. What was it like?

With the help of this last koan I will try, as best I may, to show what course the meditant follows, and what is the point of the exercise.

For hours, days, and weeks the pupil meditates on his task. Sunk in profound concentration, he thinks the problem through in all possible directions. One thing is clear; since only two hands striking together can produce a sound, the answer can only be: No one, with the best will in the world, can hear the sound of one hand. But the

[1] Called a *shippei*. In the old days the Masters carried it with them as a wanderer's staff, but later as an emblem of their status. For variants of this koan, see *Zen and Japanese Culture*, by D. T. Suzuki, Routledge & Kegan Paul, 1959, p. 7.

[2] The most important Japanese Zen Master, who systematized the method of koan meditation.

solution cannot be as simple as that. Would it not be more cautious to say: A single hand does not emit a sound that is perceptible to the human ear? But that does not get him any further. Obviously, the point is not the sound and its audibility, which are thrown in just to make the problem more complicated. The point is obviously: What is the significance of one hand in contradistinction to two? Is not this the same as the fundamental distinction between unity and duality? The hand must be a symbol of the principle: 'One without a second.' This solution recommends itself to the pupil because it is a distinction that plays a crucial role in Buddhism and is so often discussed.

Having found such an admirable solution, the pupil hurries off to the Master. He has the right to ask him one question a day. He propounds his solution with pride and enthusiasm. The Master hears him out, shakes his head, and sends the bewildered pupil back to the meditation hall without a word. But it sometimes happens that he does not let the pupil utter a word and sends him away when he has scarcely opened the door. The pupil, thrown back on himself, begins to concentrate anew. He will distinguish himself yet, astonish the Master. Meditating doggedly, he tries to force a solution. But however he twists and turns it, he can come to no other conclusion. Why, then, did the Master dismiss him? Perhaps he only expressed himself badly? He turns the formulation over in his mind. Once more he goes to the Master, who dismisses him again, this time with evident disapproval. But again the pupil fails to discover where he has gone wrong. He now gets into a state. If he is so far from the solution, will he ever be able to reach the goal? He pulls himself together. It is a matter of life and death! With passionate energy he throws himself on the problem, not with the discriminating intellect, but with the combined forces of body, soul, and spirit, so that it never lets him alone. It torments him during recreation, at meal times, at his daily work. It pursues him even in sleep. No need now to force himself to think about it! Even when he wants distraction, *it* goes on thinking in him. All in vain; the solution just will not come. He doubts his own ability, begins to despair, and does not know where to turn. He is saved from utter despair only by the Master's admonition that he is to increase the concentration until he is no longer disturbed by moody thoughts. He must learn to wait, patiently and trustfully, until the solution is ripe and comes of its own accord, without being forced.

So now he sets about it a different way. It is no longer necessary to analyze the problem and think it out: he has done enough of that already. He no longer thinks in a circle, of this or that, of one hand or two hands, of principles and suchlike; he does not even think about the solution in order to force it, and yet he is constantly related to it in an extraordinary spiritual tension. He longs for it like a man thirsting for a quenching drink. But he behaves like a man who is trying to remember something. He feels like a person who is seeking something he has forgotten, something he has to remember at any cost, because his life depends on it.

In this state of spiritual tension, it may happen that the solution will suddenly come to him, quite unexpectedly. Or else a shout, a loud noise, or, in obstinate cases—as used to be done in earlier times —a painful blow will bring the tension to bursting point. How exciting is this moment! The pupil trembles, breaks out in a sweat. But rapturous too: what he has sought in vain comes to him in a flash. He now sees clearly where everything was a tangle before; he can see the wood in spite of the trees. The scales fall from his eyes. He feels saved. The moment is brief, like a flash of lightning, yet profoundly impressive. No wonder he cannot grasp it.

SATORI

In this frame of mind he goes to the Master, no

longer proud and enthusiastic, but embarrassed and uncertain. He keeps silent, knowing he cannot say what is boundlessly clear to him himself. Or else he stammers out something incoherent, unwilling to offer it as a solution.

The Master looks through him at once. Possibly he knew, as soon as the pupil opened the door, that this was the real thing: *satori*, enlightenment. He calms and strengthens him.

What has happened? The pupil has not found any new interpretation, any new thought. Rather, in a flash of enlightenment, he has come to the solution as if a new, spiritual eye had been let into his head. The things he sees are no different from before, he just sees them differently. His vision— as well as perhaps he himself—has changed.

Hence there is no direct way from the ordinary mode of seeing and apprehending to this new vision conditioned by *satori*. It is more like jumping into a new dimension. Accordingly this new vision cannot be compared to anything and is, strictly speaking, indescribable.

But is there no hope even of hinting at its characteristics? If not, there would be nothing but a vacuum, and everything that logically follows from this vision would be more incomprehensible than ever. For later and higher stages of Zen have their roots in his fundamental intuition, in this realization at first glance. And so, for those who cannot go the way of Zen themselves and know about it only from hearsay, an attempt must be made to describe the vision somehow, however inadequately. But—the finger pointing at the moon is not the moon itself, as the Zen Masters rightly observe.

Suzuki is very much aware of the need to do this. He calls it 'an illuminating insight into the very nature of things'.[1] 'Satori is a sort of inner perception—not the perception, indeed, of a single individual object but the perception of Reality itself, so to speak.'[2] 'Perception of the highest order.'[3] 'If we want to get to the very truth of things, we must see them from the point of view where this world has not yet been created, where the consciousness of this and that has not yet been awakened.'[4]

These remarks are undoubtedly correct, but they are as enigmatic as *satori* itself. There is a danger of their activating the reader's fantasy and powers of reflection, so that he will form a mental picture which, no matter how it turns out, will always be misdrawn. I will therefore try a different approach, in the hope of conveying a few hints.

The first characteristic, it seems to me, of the

---

[1] *An Introduction to Zen Buddhism*, London, n.d. (1948), p. 47.
[2] p. 93.   [3] p. 109.   [4] p. 52.

new way of seeing is that all things are of equal importance in its sight, the most trivial as well as the most significant by ordinary human standards. They all seem to have acquired an absolute value, as if they had become transparent, revealing a relationship which does not obtain in the ordinary field of vision. This relationship is not horizontal, linking one thing to another and so remaining within the world of objects, but vertical: it plumbs each single thing to its very depths, to the point of origination. Things are thus seen, and at the same time understood, from the origin, out of the 'being' which manifests itself in them. To that extent they are all of equal rank, all possessing the illustrious patents of their origin. They are not objects isolated in themselves; they point beyond themselves, to the common ground of their being, and yet this ground can be perceived only through them, through what exists, although it is the origin of all existence.

Let us be quite clear about one thing: there is not the slightest trace of reflection in this way of seeing, nor does it come about with its secret collaboration. It is not that the vision is expected, wished for, assumed to exist as a result of prolonged meditation on the koan, so that in the end you 'believe' you see your own assumption. Rather, the vision comes upon you like a flash of lightning, at a single stroke. It is so physically clear that it brings with it absolute certainty, so that you instantly 'see' and understand that things *are* by virtue of what they are *not*, and that they owe their being to this not-being which is their ground and origin.

Perhaps an anecdote, often used as a koan, will explain what is meant:

One day as Hyakujo stepped out of the house with his Master, Baso, they saw a flight of wild geese. Baso asked: 'Where are they flying?' 'They have already flown away, Master.' Suddenly Baso seized Hyakujo by the nose and twisted it. Overcome by pain, Hyakujo cried out: 'O, oh!'

'You say they have flown away,' said Baso, 'but they have all been here from the beginning.'[1]

Then Hyakujo's back ran with sweat, and he had *satori*.

The difference between these two statements is so enormous that they cannot be reconciled with one another. 'They have flown away' is a self-evident statement of ordinary common sense. They are no longer visible, they have disappeared somewhere, hence they are no longer here and are not present for me. No illumination is needed to establish that fact.

Baso sees quite differently.

[1] Cf. Suzuki, *Zen and Japanese Culture*, p. 8.

Seeing with your natural eyes, which everyone possesses from birth, can only mean registering what comes before your eyes at any moment, out of all that exists. In order for something to come before your eyes, it must exist. With the 'third' eye, which is acquired only when one is 'reborn', you see just this existence of something that is, the ground of its being. Therefore the statement must be: 'They have always been here'—naturally not at this point of space, as space and time have no part in this vision. What is bound to appear senseless, perverse, a poor joke, is thus in reality a quite simple statement of fact—a fact which Baso sees as clearly and as corporeally as Hyakujo sees the fact that the geese have flown away. Neither of these facts refutes the other, as they belong to totally different dimensions, and Hyakujo would never have been able to find the solution by prolonged reflection. Only at the moment of acute pain, which stopped him from thinking, did he find the solution through *satori*.

Now, though you may have the feeling that you could get something out of this statement of Baso's, understand it in some way and thus justify it, you must not imagine that you can adopt Baso's standpoint and project something meaningful, possibly even profound, into his statement. That is not the point at all: everything depends on your 'seeing', as Baso did, at the first glance, with an immediacy of vision which is so and not otherwise. Baso, for his part, naturally understood Hyakujo's statement; he once shared this point of view and regarded it as normal. But he also understood that it is unspiritual and eccentric.

It would be a misunderstanding to think that the illuminating vision, though it may bring a fundamental gain, nevertheless involves a grave loss; that it overlooks the bodily fullness of existence here and now, which is thus robbed of its meaning. For, important as it is to see things in the light of their illustrious origin, it is equally important to accept them simply as they are; to perceive not only that something manifests itself in them, but the form in which it is manifested.

This objection does not hit the mark. Precisely because the illuminating vision does not inquire what meaning the 'seen' might have in relation to the seer, it permits each existent to be its true self, according to its origin. It grasps things as they are 'meant to be'.

For, to the degree that their formless origin is inaccessible and inconceivable, things in their concrete forms become the more accessible to us. Bathed in the light of their origin, they themselves are illuminated. The more mysterious their ground, the more revealingly do they stand before us. The more silent they are about the ultimate questions, the less silent are they about themselves. This enables the visionary to let them go their own way without saddling them with his own preoccupations. Far from taking them as mere manifestations of a primal Ground, which at this state is inaccessible and incomprehensible, he lets each thing be itself. The peculiar quality of his selfless vision enables him to do this to an astonishing degree: as if he were right outside the bounds of animate nature, he enjoys the most intimate contact with things and their fate, even with those that seem wholly absorbed in their material existence. Occasionally he can intensify this contact to the point of complete union. It then seems to him that things do not come to him in his vision, but that they come to themselves, and that only then do they attain full reality, as if Being were beholding itself in everything that is, as if it embraced and sustained the process of seeing. He then no longer feels himself as the subjective pole, confronted by things as objects; he feels Being as the one pole, of an essentially inconceivable nature, and himself, together with everything that happens, as the other pole of concrete existence, which, like himself, proceeds from the origin.

For what applies to each and every thing applies also to the so-called ego. In this vision the ego, too, becomes transparent, even to the ultimate depths in which it is grounded. Here we may recall the koan: Show me your original face before you were born—that is, before you existed as an individual ego, as this particular person, in the world of multiplicity and oppositeness.

Again the solution of the koan consists in 'seeing' the original face with your spiritual, third eye, *finding* it rather than *inventing* it with the aid of reflection. What you then experience in regard to your own ego is not transferred by analogy to other egos, still less to things; all these other forms are directly experienced too, each by itself, from the origin.

It may be that this kind of seeing is a repetition, a revival—in intensified form—of an attitude which sometimes came naturally to us in childhood. Then, the thing we were playing with was experienced truly as itself, without our being related to it in any way, so that it seemed as if all the action proceeded from it and it were playing with us. However that may be, and whether *satori* is a reversion to the past or a completely new and unique happening, it is without doubt a tremendously powerful experience of the Absolute and Undifferentiated, summoning up all one's subjective forces and putting them at its service; it is vision, experience, penetration, and being penetrated in one. It is therefore understandable that the Zen Masters permit, at the very most, exclamations like 'Stick!' 'Snow!' 'Wild geese!' but consider the statements 'This is a stick', 'Those are wild geese' just as fallacious as the reverse, 'This is not a stick', 'Those are not wild geese', and 'The wild geese have flown away' just as fallacious as 'They have not flown away'.

A person who judges in this manner, who isolates things both from himself and from one another, breaking up the whole, is no longer a 'seer' but an observer, who stands outside the picture and experiences the observed as an opposite. He does not feel one with what he sees, he is addressed by things as if from the outside, and in turn questions them so that they shall answer. In this game of question and answer he fancies he has grasped the full reality of the 'object' and exhausted it, not noticing that he must be content with the merest substitute. Between himself and the object there is interposed a mirror-image which he crams with meaning, not realizing that for the seer his vision is overflowing with meaning, and that he has only to keep himself open to receive it.

For an observer, consciously relating everything to everything else, past and future are clearly divided in everything he perceives. Vision is not like this; it consists in a non-related present, in an unreflected Now of timeless occurrence. The rhythm is not felt as anything extraneous, but as one's own, pulsing together with all things in an inexhaustible and boundless process of change.

If, therefore, the Zen Masters discountenance any statements about the illuminating vision, it is not because they recommend a return to the mental primitiveness of the immature. What they require is not only the attainment of the 'original mind', but its conservation. This original state is not primitive, however simple and simple-minded it may look; it is the product of unceasing spiritual discipline, and it leads to a freedom to which, in truth, nothing is impossible. But it is not in the spirit of Zen to demand this antilogical attitude on principle and to apply it forcibly to all spheres of life. 'Principles' of any kind are foreign to Zen. Not only is it admitted that there are spheres of life in which assertions, judgments, plans, and purposeful actions play a part, but Zen even goes so far as to acknowledge that these modes of behaviour are necessary to existence, thus justifying the destruction of the primal unity, the split into subject and object—but only up to the point where it threatens danger and disaster.

FURTHER KOAN MEDITATIONS

At the appropriate time, the Master will entrust more koans to his pupil. Not in order to complete the enlightenment bit by bit—for it is imparted at one stroke and as an indivisible whole, since the whole of Zen is contained in each koan—but to make the process of enlightenment more familiar, to let it take root, to exercise it. At the same time it is possible to explore the whole range of being with the help of koans; they can even be classified in this respect.

At this stage the pupil will not repeat the old mistakes when meditating. He does not look now for any rational solution, having learned by his previous failures that thinking is totally useless and must be eliminated. It is possible that he has hardly begun meditating when the solution comes to him at first go; it positively leaps at him and he 'sees' in a flash what was asked. He will then turn to the Master, and his solution will be either confirmed or rejected. He submits to the Master's decision, not just in the spirit of humility and obedience, bowing to decisions which he thinks are wrong, but in full assent, as if to the decrees of fate. This docility may not have been in him from the beginning. There may be times when he rebels against the Master's claim to see through him, until one day he realizes how wrong he was. After that, he submits willingly and has unshakeable confidence in the Master.

HOW THE MASTER SEES WHETHER THE PUPIL HAS SATORI

Whence does the Master obtain this authority, which he neither seeks nor demands, but which grows upon him despite himself? How is it possible for him to gaze into his pupil's very soul, when he stands struck dumb in his presence, or muttering helplessly? How does he know and see whether the pupil has attained *satori*? It is as difficult to explain this as the process of *satori* itself.

We must emphasize again that the illuminating vision is of such a nature that the pupil cannot give an articulate answer to the question contained in the koan, since it is impossible to express it in verbal concepts. But even supposing that he could describe the vision with the help of analogies (which might be possible after some years, with increasing experience), it would not impress the Master. For the pupil might only be repeating what he had heard from others, in order to simulate a genuine experience. With a very vivid imagination and a few facts at his disposal, he could put together the essential features of the vision and, merely because he could express it in words, pretend to be one who had experienced *satori*.

In order to take the wind out of these opportunists, who are to be found in Zen as elsewhere, the Master demands to 'see' with his own eyes the pupil's attainment of *satori*. And he, the Master of *satori*, does in fact see with unerring glance. His own experiences as a pupil enable him to do this, then his years of experience as a teacher and finally as a Master. But what does the Master see? Perhaps I can get around this question by an analogy: it is like a painter who, by glancing at the work of his students, is able to tell which of them are born artists and which are not. He just 'sees' this, but how he sees it can never be explained or taught to a non-painter. Similarly, the Zen Master sees when *satori* is genuine and not merely imagined. Naturally, he sees it 'by' something, and although I cannot explain how he does this, I will try to give a few hints which may prove helpful.

The state of mental relaxedness which results from *satori* and which brings about a profound inner transformation is reflected in a relaxedness of the body. Characteristically, *satori* does not induce any striking buoyancy of being, a sense of excitement or a general feeling of elation—

phenomena which may have quite other causes—for the enlightened one is serene and not in any way conspicuous. The effects of *satori* show themselves, rather, in his most inconspicuous movements which are least subject to his control. These movements cannot be imitated, for in Zen there are no typical attitudes that can be learned by rote, such as an attitude of devoutness, humility, ecstasy, etc. The one exception is the attitude of meditative absorption. This can be imitated for a while, but not indefinitely, because the futility of it exposes itself: it does not lead to *satori*.

I will not even lay stress on how much is betrayed by the eyes. This is true in other spheres of life, and all over the world mankind has made an art of studying the eyes. But the art of seeing, from the way a pupil raises a bowl of tea to his mouth, whether he has experienced genuine *satori* can be practised only by a Zen Master.

I will content myself with this single example: perhaps it is the most accessible to Westerners. At any rate it is quite certain that one who has experienced *satori* not only sees things differently but 'grasps' them differently, in the most literal sense of the word. But in what way does he 'grasp' them? Not because he is in the presence of the Master, awkwardly and self-consciously. Not admiring their form, appreciating their value. Not even, in the case of the bowl, *qua* bowl: the importance of the bowl depends on what is in it. Not, on the other hand, *not* noticing it, as if he were sunk in thought. But rather as a potter might grasp it, feeling how it came into being—for it tells of a master's forming hand; he grasps it as though his hands were one with the bowl, so that they themselves become like a bowl and, when he withdraws them, still seem to bear its impress. He even drinks the tea differently from other people. He drinks it in such a way that he no longer knows whether he is the drinker or the drink, completely forgetful of himself, lost to himself: the drinker one with the drink, the drink one with the drinker.

In this sense the Master's power to 'see' *satori* is simply the perfection of a faculty for which he, as an Oriental, possesses all the necessary qualifications: the faculty of detecting the finest nuances of movement and gesture. This astounding acuteness of observation may possibly have been developed by the pictographic writing, by the tendency of a Japanese to immerse himself in everything that happens, and lastly, by his love of nature. Whatever he observes enters into him—he drinks it in. We could give many examples of this attitude in Japanese life: the viewing of cherry blossom, flower exhibitions, flower arrangement, the enjoyment of landscape, of single trees. All this makes his observation of animals and people in motion more sensitive. One of the emperors was even worried by the question: With which foot does a crane start to mount a flight of steps?

It is just these insignificant, involuntary movements which are significant for the Master, as reflections of a genuine state not brought about by the will.

If my Zen Master were to read what I have just written, he would perhaps say: 'Why be so complicated about something so simple, why make so many words! To understand another person, to see into the most secret corners of his soul, is possible only through a relationship of solar plexus to solar plexus!' That is to say, with long practice you can acquire the ability to draw another person into your own field of power, which you spread around you in ever-widening rings. Not only human beings, animals, and plants, but things too. Nothing can escape it. And anything that is drawn in is bound to reveal its name and its nature.

The Master, therefore, can already see through his pupil from his outward behaviour, but still more from the way he tries to express himself when questioned. It is quite impossible for him to pretend to have something he hasn't, because there is nothing in *satori* that can be conceived and expressed as an objective fact; it contains no truths which you can pick up and say by rote, but only a new way of seeing and apprehending. Either you have *satori*, or you haven't; you cannot invent it. And anyone who has himself studied for many years under a Zen Master will no longer controvert his claim to see into the pupil's heart, to know where he stands, and above all, how much is genuine experience and how much is fantasy.

REMARKS ON JAPANESE ACTING

By way of confirmation, let us consider an art in which this feeling for expressive movement plays a crucial role: the art of acting.

The actor gains his effect not by high—and often empty—pathos, not by sweeping gestures, but by muted acting, known as the 'voiceless', 'inner' art. It does not lose itself in emotionality, and every single detail of it is perfectly formed. The spectator does not see merely the bare movement, as it were in isolation; he knows how to interpret it in relation to feelings and moods of all kinds, and he judges the greatness of an actor by his power to express himself in little. A few words, an inclination of the head, a movement of the hand, perhaps merely of a finger—that is enough for an actor to speak more eloquently than ever he could with words. The Japanese theatre, No as well as Kabuki, is based not on words but—here we can discern its Buddhist roots—on silence, so that the story can only be suggested, not told. There are plays in which the actors, without uttering a word, can hold the audience spellbound by a power of expression which is so economical that it has been called frozen dancing, or the undancing dance.

A Japanese play is not meant to be read, like a European one, which may reveal all its beauty, or brilliance, or profundity at the first reading; it 'becomes' a play only through the genius of the actor, who adds to it precisely that element which cannot be expressed by words.

While acting, his face is almost completely immobile, expressionless, with staring eyes. There should be nothing surprising in this. For one thing, masks have been used since ancient times in the No plays; for another, the actors owe a very great deal to the influence of the puppet theatre, where the power of expression resides in gestures of the most sparing kind. This has been developed to such an art that it seems to have reached perfection. Only on this basis can we understand why the tradition of the dumb-show is carefully preserved and is slowly learned from youth up (even as early as in infancy). There is in existence a theatre record begun several centuries ago, whose central feature is a pedantically accurate description of the dumb-shows performed by great actors. This was felt to be the main task and purpose of theatrical criticism. Every actor could then learn how his great predecessors played his particular role and how to work toward a truly timeless form of acting. The leading actor in Tokyo today was taught by his father: 'Above all, no originality.' That is the concern of a mediocre actor. It is easy to appear spectacular, but the good actor strives to be as unspectacular as possible.

The result, not surprising in the circumstances, is a theatre *sub specie aeternitatis*. Every movement, however trivial, means something, especially in the No plays. The tiniest variations and shades of meaning give rise to different schools of acting—something that is almost inconceivable with us. This is possible only because these momentous gestures have been brought to final perfection, so that even the smallest variation counts. The reason why they do not have the effect of stereotypes despite the formal underlying pattern, and why they do not degenerate into a routine of which even mediocre actors could avail themselves, is that in Japan nature, life, and art flow into one another without a break. Art is not a realm of appearance apart from and above nature and life, it is the perfection of them— through the artist, who has supreme control of technique and is thereby liberated from it.

The art of Japanese acting must remain largely inaccessible to the European, not merely because he does not know the language, but because he has not developed the Oriental's faculty of vision. Though he can follow without effort the most intricate dialogue in a European play, he is helpless when confronted with the simplest scene in a Japanese theatre or dumb-show. He cannot deny that his culture is founded on Logos, whereas the culture of the Far East is founded on intuitive vision.

Lest I be suspected of exaggerating in order to illustrate the background of *satori*, there is the famous anecdote of two great Masters of the theatre to bear me out: One of them recognized the greatness and superiority of the other by his overpoweringly impressive demeanour in a scene in which not a single word is spoken.

All this the Master possesses by virtue of having been born in the East. If, in addition, he has a third eye granted by *satori*, one can imagine what results may be achieved by this revolutionizing of his powers of vision.

TRANSFORMATION OF THE PUPIL BY SATORI

Satori brings about an inner transformation of a

revolutionary character. The pupil does not notice it at first; only his teacher notices it, and he does not discuss it, but lets it ripen and come to perfection. Gradually, however, the pupil notices the change in himself, in his relations with others. There is no longer the same spontaneous communication. But that does not shake his certainty: the vision he has gained is far too convincing. It is just that he withdraws from the others. More and more he gives himself up to his visions, and seeks and loves solitude.

What at first seemed a loss now becomes a gain. For he finds solitude not in far-off, quiet places; he creates it out of himself, spreads it around him wherever he may be, because he loves it. And slowly he ripens in this tranquillity. For the inner process that is now beginning to unfold, stillness is extraordinarily important. There is then no danger of his discussing it with others, of dissipating the seeds in talk. Not that he abandons himself to idle self-enjoyment; he wants only to clarify what has happened to him. It is as if he had to expose his illuminated vision to a vision of still greater luminosity, forever intensifying the original experience of enlightenment. It is a natural, self-perpetuating process which comes about by retaining the illuminated vision of reality in a fixed image, and then feeding the image back into vision. Again, this process is not initiated consciously, it happens of itself.

It is the way into art, and ultimately it becomes a way of art.

Herein lies the difference between Zen in the individual arts and the method of Zen. Physical and mental relaxedness is also the aim in the individual arts, and the inner transformation this brings about. But it is not so radical as in Zen itself. Exaggerated ego impulses are suppressed but not completely denied. Yet each of these arts points beyond itself and is a way to Zen, to the 'artless art' which Zen perfects, making use of their results for its own fulfilment.

ZEN PAINTING

This is not the place to discuss the abiding influence which Zen has had on all the Japanese arts, as Suzuki has shown, nor the method of instruction in the individual arts, the need for concentration, and the inner work by means of which the artist becomes a Master. I have done this in my other book, *Zen in the Art of Archery*, where I was concerned with the influence of Zen as a whole on the individual arts, including the art of swordsmanship.

Here we are concerned with something else: the

specific influence of *satori*, the way in which it expresses itself pictorially, above all in Zen painting. For there is a distinct school of Zen painting: works in which the illuminated vision of existence is the theme of the picture.

What is characteristic of these paintings? First of all, space. But space in Zen painting is not our Western space with its various dimensions—a uniform medium in which things stand, which surrounds them and isolates them from one another. Not a dead emptiness which can be displaced by objects and is confined to the visible relations between right and left, top and bottom, foreground and background. Not a space that touches only the surface of the object, enclosing it like a skin, and therefore, where there is nothing in it, void of meaning, an undemanding background. Space in Zen painting is forever unmoved and yet in motion, it seems to live and breathe, it is formless and empty and yet the source of all form, it is nameless and yet the reason why everything has a name. Because of it things have an absolute value, are all equally important and meaningful, exponents of the universal life that flows through them. This also explains the profound significance, in Zen painting, of leaving things out. What is not suggested, not said, is more important and expressive than what is said.

Here again, as in the art of the theatre, you see the 'undancing dance' animating all existence, pervading and dancing through all things. Space is not a homogeneous, empty medium extending to infinity; it is the inconceivable plenitude of existence itself, with all its infinite possibilities. The Zen painter therefore has no *horror vacui*; for him the Void is worthy of the highest veneration; it is the most living thing of all, so overflowing with life that it need not assume shape and form and, in order to become manifest, particularize itself in the endless cycle of change. Space is not the skin lying around things, but their core, their deepest essence, the reason for their being. The magic of the Void is expressed in these paintings, bewitching the eye, summoning a mood of reverence. Looking at painting always begins with looking at the Void.

In Western painting the observer stands outside the picture. What he sees is experienced as an opposite, living its own separate life and carrying his eye in diminishing perspective to the horizon. It is as though the mere act of looking were creative. For this mode of seeing everything opposite is essentially extraneous, outside the observer, and it enters into his consciousness by the very fact that he is not there, but is detached from the picture. In Chinese and Japanese painting you do not look in from outside at an opposite, for the subject and every detail of it are seen so intensely from the inside that the beholder must himself be in the picture, must live in it, in order to do it justice. Not only does perspective become so pointless that it disappears altogether, but the relation of observer to observed is abolished. Space closes around the observer, who now stands everywhere in the centre without being the centre: he is now in their midst, one with the heartbeat of things. And in turn, what surrounds and encloses him is so much his own equal that he feels it is not there for him and for his sake. It is not an opposite but, as it were, himself in ever-changing form. They are so at one that he no longer has a meaning of his own; he is submerged in it and, vanishing within it, encounters himself and yet not himself: an evanescence in the essence of things.

But the objects in the picture, mountains and woods, rocks, and water, flowers, animals, and men—forms sprung from the Void—stand there fully revealed in their actuality, plunged in the concrete situation of the Here and Now—and yet not in a mere Here and Now. Hence the impression of continual evanescence, as though the definite were being absorbed back into the indefinite, the formed into the formless, thus making visible the primal Ground from which they come.

There are textbooks of ink painting in which

everything that the painter's eye can meet—from a blade of grass to a great landscape—is held fast in its essential features, capturing in a few strokes just that quality which gives nature the character of being alive. They are not intended as models to be copied, much as one is tempted to do so. Rather, they are exercises in the various styles of brush stroke, showing the close affinities between painting and calligraphy. If these exercises can be mastered so that you rise above technique into freedom, able to perceive and express the finest nuances, you are then in a position to depict what the third eye sees and interprets.

Zen painting links up with a great tradition— with Chinese landscape painting before the advent of Buddhism. There the features characteristic of Zen painting were already crystallized, or at any rate prefigured. This may perhaps have been due to the profound and secret influence of Taoism. When Buddhism first reached China from India, with revolutionary results, it underwent a slow but far-reaching transformation through Taoism. Just as China, in the course of her history, has always swallowed up the alien tribes that invaded the country, so, spiritually, she has assimilated everything that was once of foreign origin, only to give it back greatly refined and enriched. Zen is perhaps the most beautiful and most mysterious blossom of the uncanny creativity of the Chinese genius. Hence it is not surprising that Zen painters trace their descent from the pre-Buddhist paintings of China which were moulded by the spirit of Taoism. In the Taoism of Lao-tzu we find many motifs that are of fundamental importance in Zen. In fact, what was dimly discerned in Taoism is revealed in Zen.

What is true of landscape painting in general is true also of the tiniest segment of a landscape or of nature—of those incredibly alive paintings that conjure up, with a few delicate or powerful brush-strokes, a bamboo stem, a cluster of reeds, a flowering branch. They, too, are seen from the formless Void and can be understood only from that standpoint. Here again the relationship of the drawing to empty space is paramount; indeed, the peculiar feeling of space is expressed even more convincingly than in the larger compositions. Nothing could be more mistaken than to see the calm beauty of existence permanently captured there and offered for ceaseless contemplation. A person who really knows how to read this picture-writing feels, through the semblance of calm, the mighty tension of the world-process, of things rising up and sinking away, appearing and vanishing; how everything that has become vibrates in the flux of Becoming and Unbecoming—evanescent, yet absolute.

These quite simple pictures, showing so infinitely little, are so full of Zen that the beholder feels overwhelmed by them. Anyone who has seen, at a long-drawn-out tea ceremony, how the whole atmosphere changes when the hanging scrolls are put up, how the guests, sunk in contemplation before the picture, experience an unveiling of mysteries which none of them can put into words, and depart from the tea room feeling unutterably enriched, will know what power emanates from these paintings.

SATORI IN POETRY

That *satori* has also found expression in poetry can be mentioned only in passing. The short poem, or *haiku*, is particularly suited to the nature of Zen because, like ink painting, it stresses relation to space not only outwardly, in the linear arrangement, but inwardly too, in its intrinsic form. The really important things are left out, and can be read only between the lines, as in the famous poem by Basho:

> *The old pond:*
> *A frog jumps in,—*
> *The sound of the water.*[1]

[1] From R. H. Blyth, *Haiku*, vol. 1, p. 340. Kamakura, 1949.

That is all. And yet, is not the whole universe contained in it? Suddenly, in the midst of motion-less calm—movement, life, spreading rings of sound, then vanishing again. And what is all this commotion compared with the voice of silence, which is the beginning and the end?

If the painter or poet, the actor or archer, were asked how to express in a word what it is that gives life and breath to all living things, what sustains them in the 'undancing dance' of coming-to-be and passing away, he would probably answer: 'It.' In all action and non-action, 'It' is there by not being there. This is a clumsy but perhaps the closest description of what it is whose form is not this and not that, but whose hidden essence is active in all forms that are.

SPECULATION ON THE BASIS OF SATORI

For those who are unable to express themselves as painters or poets, however many attempts they have made (and later rejected), there remains the saving path of reflection—indeed, of speculation. The direction it may take, and also its goal, are illustrated in these excerpts from *The Five Steps of Tosan Ryokai:*

Speculation on the Basis of Satori

FIRST STEP

At the third night-watch or at the first
Before the moon is out,
Who can be surprised if people
Pass each other by unrecognizing?
And yet there remains a hidden
Trace of the day that has gone.

SECOND STEP

An old woman who has ignored the morning
Stands opposite the ancient mirror.
They reflect each other in perfect clarity,
There is no longer anything real.
Stop going out of your mind again
And giving substance to shadows!

Tosan Ryokai (ninth century) wants to say something like this: The illuminating vision is such that the individual differences of the day vanish in the night of undifferentiated Sameness, the formless Ground and matrix of all being. This undifferentiated Sameness is that mysterious 'It' which has been so incontrovertibly experienced. The differences disappear, yet they are not completely abolished in the sense of being annihilated—transformed back into Nothing. They are only negated in thought, in order to make the undifferentiated Sameness thinkable. Anyone who ignores the morning, which brings back the opposites into

59

which the undifferentiated Sameness is polarized, stands opposite truth as opposite a mirror. He cannot get away from the thought of 'It', the formless Nothing. Himself grown old (for he has entered into the timeless night of truth), he stands opposite Nothing, still as 'one' confronting the 'other'. But always there are two: the mind that thinks the thought of Nothing, and Nothing as the truth that is thought.

Anyone, therefore, who supposes he has attained the highest truth in the thought of Nothing, wherein all differences are extinguished, and believes that he is superior to those artists who do not get beyond seeing, in the things of the day, the undifferentiated Sameness, in all appearances the illustrious origin, and in all forms the formless Ground —who, in a word, does not think 'abstractly' enough—such a person, according to Ryokai, is in danger of going out of his mind. He does not realize that the Nothing he thinks he has attained is only the shadow of the truth, not truth itself. For this Nothing is still, and always must be, a distinction predicated by the mind: it is the opposite of This and That, of the One in contradistinction to the Many; it is a product of intellectual effort and therefore an empty nothing, a figment of the brain. This is where speculation, pure thinking, leads.

The Master has nothing against these efforts, even though the koan exercise ought really to have driven out thought. For him reflection is a point of transition. Forbidding it will not stop it. He leaves the artist with his pictures, the thinker with his thoughts, knowing that the way goes onward and contains its own correction.

THE ROLE OF THOUGHT IN ZEN

It is impossible for the intellect to conceive, even with the boldest constructions of thought, something that is bestowed and immediately apprehended only by means of the original mystical experience. It is only afterward, in the wake of the experience, that the Zen Buddhist will concede that the mystical content becomes accessible to the intellect. But the statements that then emerge are of use only to one who has had the experience, and he can do without them. Lacking this, anyone who tries to appropriate them will be thrown into confusion and despondency, and for him they work like poison.

Thus, the contrasting of multiplicity with unbroken unity, of difference with identity, of oppositeness with non-oppositeness, would also have a sound and conceptually legitimate meaning for the

Zen Buddhist. But, in view of his experiences, he is not prepared to regard the non-opposite, the undifferentiated and identical One as *more original* than the opposite, the differentiated, and the manifold, and on that account to load it with mystical honours. For him, too, the non-opposite is beyond all conceivable opposites, yet precisely for that reason it is still an opposite, still the pole of a tension out of which the postulated non-oppositeness does not lead. If he deigned to express an opinion on the theme of non-oppositeness at all, he would probably say: The centre of being is *beyond* all opposites just because it dwells within them, and *within* all opposites just because it 'is' beyond them. It is without contradiction and yet full of contradictions. Or, to put it another way: One and Many, undifferentiated and differentiated, non-opposite and opposite are equally near and equally far from the centre of being, they are the centre of being itself and, in the same breath, are not.

Such formulations are impenetrable and meaningless for anyone who seeks salvation on no other path than that of thought. But anyone who has experienced the centre of being with his own body will be able to plumb its very depths in the space of one long exhalation, and will cease to wonder why anything so simple and obvious cannot be communicated except in obscure formulas. He will then understand why the Zen Masters not only avoid all talk but regard it as dangerous and, instead, urge the pupil toward those crucial experiences which solve all riddles at one stroke.

ZEN IN PRACTICAL LIFE

However revolutionary the spiritual transformation may be which the pupil experiences through *satori*, the whole of him is not, to begin with, included in this transformation. Though he is spiritually free, he is still far from being free in that inclusive sense which would enable him to live by the truth, and by this alone. For this truth—if such 'It' may be called—is not yet in sight; he is only moving toward it. He sees what underlies all things, himself included, but always he is something other than what he sees: he is not yet one with his own ground, or rather, with the unfathomability of that ground.

Everyone who has experienced *satori* is painfully aware of this as soon as he puts the quiet meditation room behind him in order to take up his profession again, or start work of some kind. Naturally, there are frictions in a monastery: the envy of the ambitious, different levels of capacity and attainment. But the presence of the Master restores the balance, so the prevailing atmosphere is one of harmony and forbearance. Outside the monastery life begins in earnest, assaulting senses which in the meantime have become doubly sensitized. Once more you are in a world of aims and intentions. The intellect, hitherto switched off, once more takes pride of place and is used as a tool.

Even the artist, though he may have become without purpose in his particular sphere, is not spared this contact with life—and how much less is anybody else? Even lay priests are drawn into it. They marry, thereby—especially in the Far East—involving themselves in a multitude of obligations which weigh them down. Gone is the unpurposing existence in the shelter of the monastery! A gulf opens out between everyday life and a life of seclusion. All of them meet with conditions they find irksome, even though they are content to stay in their allotted places and have no wish to advance themselves or play a role in public life. They do not advocate forcible reforms; they wait patiently in the conviction that there is room enough in the world for the old and the new, that the old will disappear when it is time, and that the new does not arrive ready-made but grows out of the seeds of the old. Therefore they try to be of service un-criticizingly, selflessly, not adapting things to themselves but themselves to things, and paying attention less to what they do than to how they do it, letting things be and trying to make the best of them.

On the quiet they work at themselves. With others they are indulgent, with themselves not. They begin in a small and modest way, knowing that only so can they master greater difficulties.

Their monastic training has left its mark and conditions their attitude to others: not to complain about people and circumstances, not to change them but to change themselves, and to develop countervailing forces. A sensitive conscience develops too—they are scrupulously honest with themselves. This does not lead to self-esteem and self-righteousness. They know the advantage they have over others but take no credit for it. They are thankful to fate, and face with humility the way that lies before them. If conflicts arise they go to the Master. Whenever possible they attend further courses in meditation in order to deepen and broaden their vision. Daily meditation goes without saying. These exercises have to be continued throughout life. It is a mistake to think that they are useful only in the training period and can then be set aside. The Master also must constantly repeat his exercises, not in order to attain at-one-ment but to consolidate what has been attained. Meditation is thus of absolutely central importance.

Everything that has been achieved is merely a preliminary exercise for achievements to come, and no one—not even one who has reached perfection—can say he has reached the end.

ZEN PRIESTS

It is hardest of all for the young priest. He is conscious of the long and arduous way that lies ahead of him, and he wants to make progress to the limit—that is, to the limit of his capacity. All his powers are concentrated on that goal. And now, instead of working toward the fulfilment of his own life, he has to care for the salvation of others! He would willingly do so when he himself could draw strength from fulfilment. But the moment seems premature. He, too, is only a beginner.

It seems to him very hard to be reminded of his vow to save others. He is called upon to leave the house of fruitful solitude, and to mingle in the distractions of a life he has renounced. For, unlike the others who go out into life after experiencing *satori*, the young priest cannot be content to exercise quiet and unobtrusive influence in the station to which he has been called. He must penetrate into alien regions and mix with people whose company everyone would wish to avoid.

Here he is put to a painful test, meeting with anything from polite indifference to outright rejection, contempt, and derision. He even meets with hatred—hatred born of envy. Involuntarily he has to ask himself by what right he disturbs and interferes with those less privileged than himself. What has he to offer? Is he to proclaim the beatific vision, as the artist does in his paintings? Preach that man will never be free under the yoke of desire? But preaching means 'making words', and that goes against the spirit of Zen. The only thing he can do, apart from giving help in every form like a good friend and neighbour, is to show that the yoke of desire, the universal law of cause and effect, can be broken. He can show—if only the others have eyes to see—that he himself has broken the bond. And as his humility is disarming, the others do not, in fact, close their minds to him. This results in the obligation to lead an exemplary life, to hold up to others the one quality in which he excels: his unremitting work on himself. The Zen priest cannot evade his duties by mere talk. He cannot preach and demand of others tolerance, patience, mercy, and compassion unless he himself religiously fulfills these requirements. Rhetoric does not stand high on the programme in Zen.

Consequently, the Zen priest must exercise the most rigorous self-control. For him there is no such excuse as 'Oh, I just lost my temper'. Nor does he wait until he is told—by others—that he is still under the sway of desires and passions. As soon as he becomes aware of this weakness, he voluntarily breaks off his ministry and retires to meditate all the more intensively, in solitude, until he can look the world in the face again, and especially himself. Indeed, even if it means neglecting exercises which might carry him further along the path of Zen, he considers it more important to purify the springs of his being.

Nor is outward success long in coming: he is now more readily accepted. His achievement impresses people; it no longer appears as something esoteric, associated with the musty smell of monasteries and their mysterious practices. He seems more like an athlete, whose performance is within reach of anyone willing to set his mind to it and submit to the necessary training. His ministry becomes less suspect, and it is easier for him to make contact. As a result, he acquires the status of a secular teacher who helps people over their worst afflictions. But—is he not betraying his vocation? Is *satori*, the long and arduous path he has travelled, needed just for this? Is it for this that he is a Zen priest? Occasionally, therefore, besides giving help and encouragement, he will speak of the way that leads to salvation, of the liberation from desire and the value of this sacrifice. He may find a few listeners, but as a rule that is as far as it goes. He now realizes how difficult his task is.

Desires are so deeply ingrained in most human beings, take up so much room, that it does indeed seem quite hopeless. Worse still, there is not only desire to be encountered everywhere, but evil-mindedness, cruelty, malice, dishonesty. The naïve sensualists are at least uncomplicated and easy to approach; far otherwise with those malicious souls who know the distinction between good and evil and deliberately reject the good, even hate it! For the novice this is a devastating experience.

He has heard of the original Buddha nature of all things, and has glimpsed it all around him: in trees and rocks, in mountains and rivers, in flowers and bushes. Should it not be found in man as well? But here his illuminated vision fails him. He is faced with something that does not exist in the vegetable and animal kingdoms: man's abysmal mendacity. Animals do not pretend, play roles, wear masks. What has become of the Buddha nature in man? Is it not evident that his original nature is corrupt?

These misgivings end in doubt and drive the novice back to the Master for clarifying talks, which are now quite appropriate since they are concerned with difficulties that lend themselves to rational explanation. A new course of instruction begins, of indefinite duration—not always in the form of discussions, lectures, and exercises, but varying in method to suit the individuality of the pupil, and aided by selected koans which enable him to work out for himself the solution of his problems. At all events it will give guidance concerning his vocation and conduct as a priest, and deal frankly with his predicament: the difficulties of a novice who feels that to have to save others is a violation and almost a betrayal of his own nature, who is not yet driven by an inner impulse which makes concern for others perfectly natural and self-evident, and who feels as awkward as a half-trained doctor turned loose on his patients.

It now becomes clear to him that, for the time being, he cannot help feeling lost. The fault lies not with the wicked world, but with himself and his own lack of serenity. Inwardly he is still conditioned by the face the world shows to him. Failure and depression should make him conscious of this fact. It is himself that he must first put in order; failure therefore has a salutary effect. His task is to remain steadfast in heart, and to do this in his dealings with people and things is the prerequisite for saving others, which can be achieved only after a long period of trial.

On this road there are new dangers and temptations. It is inevitable that, having chosen the way of highest truth, he should endeavour to live by the truth as he sees and understands it. He lives by its principles and takes care to be, to think, and to act accordingly. He has decided for goodness and truth, and set his face against evil and untruth, without realizing that with this decision he has got himself in a fix. By discriminating between goodness and holiness on the one hand and evil and unholiness on the other, he places himself squarely on one side of an antithesis. But the *Shinjinmei* ('Treatise on Faith in Mind')[1] says:

The perfect Way (Tao) is without difficulty.
Save that it avoids picking and choosing.[2]

This 'picking and choosing' is manifest in the fact that in order to grasp one thing he must reject the other. He thus adopts an attitude, which is always one-sided. In spite of his having decided for goodness, its opposite gains power over him. By holding firmly to goodness (ideals, values) he is as much in bondage as the man who is at the mercy of his desires. Anyone who repudiates the lust for life because he is caught in the lust for ideals has

[1] Written by the third Patriarch, Sosan. The text (in a translation by Shuei Ohasama, revised by E. Herrigel) can be found in *Zen: Der lebendige Buddhismus in Japan*, by Shuei Ohasama and Augustus Faust, with a commentary by Rudolf Otto.

[2] Alan Watts, *The Way of Zen*, p. 115. London, 1957.

not advanced in the most fundamental sense. True, he is further advanced than the unthinking man of desires, since he is conscious of both sides and understands the irreconcilable tension between them. But he has not yet gone far enough: he is not yet beyond the opposites, living out of a truth that has superseded them. Therefore, he meets with rejection. The priest who sees in this only malevolence becomes all the more demanding, thinks himself superior, and is full of reproaches for the wicked and intolerant, not yet free from the desire for recognition, honour, even veneration. There is an unadmitted power-drive at work in him, and his 'cure of souls' is largely an expression of this in the guise of holy zeal and moral superiority. He is, indeed, called to leadership in the highest sense, but this leadership of which he is not yet capable springs from a different plane: it too is a power, though of an incomparably different kind. Holy zeal is not justified even when sinners mock the Buddha and the highest truth. The priest is not the advocate of this truth, so he will take care not to talk about the Buddha or Zen.

How about the evil-minded? Led astray by rationalism, they feel themselves the centre to which everything is related. This obstinate self-will causes the Buddha nature to be completely obscured in them. The illuminated vision no longer avails here; self-will appears to be man's original nature. The priest has no choice but to believe the Buddha and the Masters when they say that the Buddha nature resides even in a criminal. He must believe this until he sees it for himself and so becomes independent of the Buddha and the Masters. In order to attain this knowledge, which is like a *satori* of the highest potency, renewed exercises are required. Just as special breathing exercises and concentration were needed for *satori*, so now he must perform exercises which include the whole of his being—not only his mind, but his soul and his body. He must get beyond the opposites in which he is still caught, as a prelude to a transformation that is no longer of his own doing, but is something that 'happens' to him. His own unhappy experiences have prepared the priest for this. The essential thing is for him to become ego-less in a radical sense, so that 'ego-self' does not exist any more, either as a word or as a feeling, and turns into an unknown quantity. Ego-self, till now the secret or conscious point of reference for all everyday experiences, must vanish.

This does not mean that 'I' should be superseded and replaced by a vague 'We', for group experience still affects the individual as an ego, even if he does not react to it individually and personally but in the spirit of the group. 'I' should rather be replaced by 'It'.

The exercises, a continuation of the earlier ones, should result in complete equanimity. Everything that happens, and above all what happens to me, should be observed impartially, as though on the deepest level it did not concern me. This means rejoicing when something happens to *me* exactly as I would if it happened to someone else, and sorrowing under another's sorrow no less than if it befell me. Indeed, I must be able to rejoice over another's joy even if it brings me sorrow (when, for instance, another is preferred to me), and be troubled by another's sorrow even when the cause of his sorrow brings joy to me.

It goes without saying that a disciple of the Buddha may not hate, and in the end cannot hate. Equally, he may not love in the ordinary sense of the word, and in the end cannot do so. Yet he does not become unfeeling and indifferent. He lets everything and everybody have a share in his rich capacity for loving, without counting on any love in return. He loves impartially, selflessly, as though only for the sake of loving. And this not because it gives him personal pleasure or satisfies a personal desire, but because he must do so out of abounding love. This love, if one can call it that, since it is incapable of changing into hate, is beyond both. It is not like a leaping flame that may subside at any moment; it is like a calm radiance that perpetuates itself. This love, which can neither be disappointed nor encouraged from without, in which goodness, compassion, and gratitude are mingled, which does not woo, does not obtrude itself, make demands, disquieten, or persecute, which does not give in order to take, possesses an astounding power, precisely because it shuns all power. It is gentle, mild, and in the long run irresistible. Even so-called inert things open themselves to it, and animals, otherwise shy and distrustful, trust it.

This would explain why the Japanese love of nature is bound up with Zen. It is the purest form of a love that turns spontaneously to things and does not change into hate. Many examples of this love of nature could be given: one thinks of the Japanese attitude to flowers. This is the purest instance of love without requital: I love the flower not because it blossoms for me but because it blossoms wholly without reference to me, and I rejoice in its existence not as though it were my possession.

If you have gone through this schooling, if you have tried in some such way to reach a position beyond the opposites, you will then have fulfilled the conditions for a fruitful encounter with the 'other'; you will be able to apprehend it 'in itself', at a glance, intuitively, as an experienced doctor sums up his patient. From this vantage point a human being can be seen through just as he is, together with everything in him that is warped or perverse, no longer despised now, but calmly accepted for what it is at this moment. And as the priest's field of power gains in strength, the more impossible it becomes for the other to deceive him, to put up the barrier of a pretence. It becomes the medium in which the other involuntarily relaxes and unfolds, a beckoning centre to which he surrenders, yielding it the leadership.

The priest experiences no increase of 'himself' in this contact with the other, he only strengthens the 'It' in him. He feels borne along by forces that are other than himself.

His help for others consists in merely being there, in a not-doing, an attitude which is preeminently spiritual and uniquely creative. Body, soul, and spirit are here fused into a unity.

He works on others by his own example, and waits until they are at a loss and want advice. He will then perhaps counsel them to fulfill their duties consciously, faithfully, and selflessly. He will not talk of Zen or expect to put them on the path until the ground is prepared. Only then will he explain the fundamental error of regarding themselves as the centre to which everything must be related, of insisting on their own will and thus perverting the universal law by adjusting things to themselves instead of themselves to things. Then, in small ways, he will introduce them to the exercises he himself has gone through, carefully setting them on the path that brings release from self-will and desire.

THE CENTRE OF BEING

Egohood belongs to the very nature of man, as wings to a bird or leaves to a tree. In itself there is nothing suspect about it, nothing from which the eccentricity of human existence could be derived. Yet a falling away, a defection from the centre, is implicit in this egohood. By learning to discriminate himself more and more from everything that is not himself, that does not belong to him, man experiences the tension between ego and non-ego as an opposition. The more consciously he confronts everything not himself as an object, the more the ego places itself outside—outside what is 'opposite' to it. The result is a continuous division of being into the two realms of subjective and objective—so much so that the more the art of discrimination progresses, the more puzzling it appears how the One Being could ever have divided itself into two such different realms.

Now, however correct it may be to contrast, as a postulate, identity with difference, unity with multiplicity, the undifferentiated with the differentiated, non-oppositeness with oppositeness, there is no mystical sublimity about these pairs of opposites. The fact that the intellect cannot conceive identity-and-unity except in the medium of duality does not mean that it should be the object and theme of mystical awareness.

For the Zen Buddhist, who does not allow himself to be confused by flights of speculation, the true mystery is not only beyond all multiplicity, oppositeness, and differentiation, but also beyond the pairs of opposites 'unity : multiplicity,' 'identity : difference', 'non-oppositeness : oppositeness'. And even this is arguable, because it runs counter to certain very definite mystical experiences.

If he considered it sufficiently important to express an opinion on this problem in the terms we have used here, he would be unable to say anything more than that the centre of being is as much *beyond* unity and multiplicity, identity and difference as it is *not* beyond them. And since being beyond them and not being beyond them are again opposites, he would have to add that the centre of being is neither the one nor the other, neither both nor not both, and that it cannot be described, or even hinted at, by the processes of thought, Anyone who wishes to know what it is must follow the path of Zen—there is no other choice.

MAN'S FALL AND FULFILMENT

How, then, did man's fall come about? It began by his disregarding or misunderstanding the deepest purpose of his existence. No other creature is constituted by nature, as he is, not only to live spontaneously from the centre of being, but, in untroubled communion with the whole of life, to reveal the secret of all existence. He has been granted the ultimate possibility of bursting the bonds of his individuality, of entering into intimate contact with everything that is, of encountering everywhere in the external world something akin to him, or perceiving in this kinship himself, and in this self becoming aware of the centre of being, so that he *lives* as much as he *is lived*.

No other beings outside and below man live: they *are* lived. With the certainty of sleepwalkers they lead an existence turned in upon itself, and none of the relationships they enter into ever penetrate their consciousness. They have no way of opening themselves and remaining open, of revealing themselves and being revealed. Whatever they do or suffer is without meaning for them. Namelessly existing, they are blissfully wrapped up in themselves, but they do not attain to conscious enjoyment of their existence.

On man, however, a new and unprecedented law is enjoined: to fulfill what was promised in his nature by inclining himself to all things, and enveloping them in love where and whenever he meets them; in a love that does not reckon and calculate, but squanders itself and only grows richer and deeper in the squandering. Only in this way can he succeed in freeing himself, step by step, from the narrow prison of individuality in which he, like the animals and plants, is confined. In the end he is restored to himself as what he really is: as the heart of existence, in which Being is made manifest.

Reverence for all life is the formula of Zen Buddhism, and in this is hidden the secret of Zen.

HIGHER STAGES OF MEDITATION

By remaining 'steadfast in mind' the Zen adept has won a new basis for his life. His earlier gains have been consolidated and an inner change has taken place in him. From this vantage point new exercises in meditation may be attempted: with no definite theme, without a koan. He has got to the point where, even with no theme, his mind remains wide-awake. It is no longer directed to a set question but to something asked unspoken, to some ultimate question that cannot be put into words. It is a question, now, not of illumination through vision, but of illumination through at-one-ment.

The mind of the meditant is wide-awake. This means not just his mind but everything in him— body, senses, and mind all acting together in the field of power. He is as wide-awake as one who waits and listens, whose life depends on his listening. But not consciously listening (that would be too definite, too limiting); he listens without knowing that he listens. He is emptied of everything, yet has no consciousness of emptiness. It is a state that only a person with long practice of meditation can get into. Seen from the outside, the meditant is as if dead. Seen from the inside he is in a state of absolute freedom (emptiness), full and completely alive, tense, concentrated, yet with no tendency to release the tension in the form of images, but rather to be drawn, imageless, into the imageless field of power.

It may then happen that the meditant, now completely immersed, feels himself as in a dazzling darkness, that he experiences light-phenomena. I do not know what they mean or where they come from. But they are transient phenomena that disappear again and apparently have no significance. For they do not lead to anything. Afterwards one feels shattered, exhausted.

But then the following thing happens (how, one does not know—or did one dream it?): you are swallowed as if by a whirlpool, sucked down to endless depths, and suddenly flung out again and brought back to yourself. It is like waking up with a jerk, and it may be accompanied by an outburst of sweat. But this time you do not feel shattered. On the contrary, you feel invigorated, new-born.

Thus you are brought back to yourself and to the world. After repeated experiences you realize: What I sought lies in *myself*, and in all these *things*. The truth is *this world, this thing here, that thing there* —and yet it is *not*. Or: This thing here is the truth—and not the truth. It is something and yet not Being, it is no-thing and yet not Nothing. It is Being and Nothing, Nothing and Being: each is right, each is wrong, as soon as it is thought and uttered.

Thought bogs down, ties itself in knots. At an

earlier stage it seemed as if the opposite and the non-opposite were two different things, regions apart! Now you have found, by experience, that the non-opposite 'is' as little as the opposite. Neither exists for itself, each exists through the other. This is neither pantheism nor deism, implying neither a God who is immanent in the world nor one who transcends it.

And everything is now as simple and easy to understand as a game; you are in full possession of sovereign freedom. This freedom does not mean being untouched by joy and suffering, love and hate, but feeling both of them intensely and yet remaining independent, not losing yourself in them, not being consumed by them. That is the difference between Zen and the life-denying attitude of the Stoic: in Zen you are above it all and in it all, and again not. Anyone who has got as far as that, will be neither purified by suffering nor destroyed by hate, neither benefited by joy nor rewarded by love. He *is* rewarded, in that it is not *he* who is rewarded. The tenor of his being is sheer goodness—the only thing that increases the more it is squandered—serenity, confidence, buoyancy. Everything that comes is right. He lives an exactingly unexacting life: like an ordinary person and yet in all things extraordinary, because in all things different. He acts rightly by instinct. He is not vain of his modesty. He has no complexes, can live from day to day and find complete fulfilment in each, quietly leaving the future in the darkness of fate.

Thus he becomes a personality by being impersonal. He has no fear of death, for he has annihilated himself so often. And he knows that in death also he will be *sublatus*, *elevatus*, and *conservatus*—annihilated, exalted, and preserved (as a field of power). Personal immortality has ceased to be a problem for him.

But still the end of the way has not been reached, there are still further exercises to do. The Zen Buddhist is always on the way, and it may be that new experiences will come. Supposing he is one of the exceptions to whom more is granted than to others; supposing he has conscientiously gone on with his exercises and his zeal has not fallen off. He will then reach a new mode of experience which, indefinable to begin with, proves to be qualitatively different from the preceding ones: a new way of being in nothing and of not-being in being. It is a new kind of happening, underivable from anything else, and it occurs quite spontaneously. His co-operation consists only in his readiness and receptivity.

This mysterious happening can only be hinted at, but the core of it will be missed. All images and comparisons stem from other levels of experience.

And yet the mystic would have so much to tell us, just because he has so much to keep silent about.

First of all, the technique of meditation is now so perfect that sometimes only a few minutes are needed for complete immersion and concentration. Observers have established that neither the breathing out nor the breathing in is accentuated; both are balanced and equalized. It is true spiritual breathing.

The vehemence with which you are expelled from the Void (*ek-stasis* in the true sense) is mitigated; for longer and longer periods it is possible to repose in the depths of nothingness to which you had sunk. The Void no longer appears as dazzling darkness, as palpable silence; there are no words to express it. So ineffable is it that the only appropriate comment is inviolable silence.

You then experience a gradual return to yourself. Not, as in the first stage, with a feeling of elation, so that you have first to accustom yourself to the light of day and the plurality of existence as something irksome; nor, as at the beginning of the second stage, like one wrenched out of a restless sleep, who struggles to remember something he has 'left lying on the way', as the Masters put it, and now seeks it everywhere in the things of this world. You are like one who, awaking after a deep, refreshing sleep, opens his eyes and takes it for granted that he will find his familiar world there again without a break, as though it could not be otherwise.

This, then, is the decisive thing—with no jerk, with no shock, you come back; you glide into existence as though no jump had to be made from here to there, from there to here.

This unexpected mode of experience is disturbing. You seek the cause in yourself, in insufficient concentration (the immersion comes so quickly). So you go on practising conscientiously, knowing that racking your brains does not help. You have had to accustom yourself to so much, why not to this too? But even the most carefully prepared concentration—when you guard against distraction hours beforehand—leads to no other result. The inexplicable mode of experience remains.

You cannot question your teacher, for he has dropped the reins. At best he would smilingly remark: 'The method of no-method!' So you have to rely entirely on yourself. Any further advance must be made without help or advice. Only a great Master could help, but he would refuse to do so on principle, because he would know that this is the turning point. If the pupil finds the way ahead the pinnacle will be reached. If not, he will remain a mere technician. Over and above all technique, genius must break through.

He would be infinitely alone and solitary were it not for the 'ecstatic' experience of the Void, which catches and holds him. He can only continue ahead, undesiring, unpurposing.

However, his mind is taken off this disturbance by a new experience which comes to him in the midst of everyday life, quite apart from the state of concentration, and which is even more disquieting than the previous one.

He finds he is becoming increasingly reluctant to intervene in the lives of others. It seems to him not only crude and tactless, but wrong. He develops something like an instinctive repugnance for it. His training has conditioned him to give heed to all such intimations, however faint, and not to counteract them—for instance, by an appeal to duty. He listens to a warning daimon, and senses an inner inhibition.

Why should this be? Has he wearied of his former zeal? Yet the fact remains: the more he progresses the more indifferent he becomes to baseness and meanness, and the less enthusiastic about what is good and exalted in man. He takes it all in his stride, like the weather. But why should that prevent him from helping?

This new attitude cannot be put down to a scepticism born of disillusionment, as if all effort to help had always been of transitory value. A little may rub off here and there, and when times are quiet it looks as though something lasting had been achieved. But in a crisis it is evident that man has remained unchanged—indeed, that unsuspected abysses have opened. All effort, therefore, is futile.

Nevertheless, the uneasy question arises: Why should he concern himself with improvements and changes of heart? Is not this the business of other authorities—parents, teachers? So why set up as a judge over secular institutions?

Hence there can be but one task for the Zen priest: to call forth the radical change, to facilitate it, not to meddle, and to pursue only this one goal. But—and here the inhibition makes itself sharply felt—not in the form of persuasion, insistence, and moral browbeating until the other person is caught. He no longer has the urge to be a fisher of souls, as if merit attached to the act of salvation and to the number of souls saved.

Help—but only by not turning to others, only by waiting until they seek my help of their own accord, until a little spark of longing flares up in them for a life in freedom and in the spirit, outshining their self-will. I do not give them what is mine, but what is theirs. It is as if *they* were availing themselves of my spiritual forces to become free: it is not I, but they, who intervene in their own existence, cut into their own flesh. Not my words, not my deeds, but my mere existence must convince them. The more undesiring and unpurposing I become, the more irresistibly do I draw these in whom—though they may not know it—the secret longing burns. But once they have made contact, they cannot draw back. It is as if a power, lord of us both, seized the other person through me, directed him to me, drew him toward me. This alone leads us together and establishes a genuine contact, a contact in depth. Then there is no deception and no disappointment. Then a lasting change is called forth, not just a passing mood.

Ever sharper and more compelling grows the realization that being changed does not depend on the will, either of the helper or of the helped, but is destiny, fate. To one it is granted, in spite of himself; another fails, despite heroic efforts.

Thus the disinclination to intervene does not mean callously leaving people to their own devices, but helping by not helping, convincing by not convincing. Only then does help become masterly. This was the kind of help the pupil once received from his teacher.

This new experience would remain incomprehensible and disquieting did it not go hand in hand with another one, somewhat less drastic, which serves to clarify the structure of that experience.

The Zen priest's attitude to everything has always been characterized by a renunciation of all categories of judgment. This is understood from the start. To be able to accept, with complete equanimity, the pleasant and the unpleasant (though the pleasant remains as pleasurable as ever, but is accepted like the weather), has always been rated a fundamental capacity which cannot be exercised enough. It has laid the foundation of a markedly impersonal and objective type of behaviour. The capacity to discover, in purely receptive vision, the essential character of an event or object has been mentioned before, and its significance for the arts has been stressed. But such an attitude has long existed outside Buddhist mysticism and is therefore not exclusive to Zen. The calm rejection of all judgments is but a preliminary stage to a highly characteristic attitude of decisive importance. Negatively one can say that it lies beyond subjective-objective, personal-impersonal. The percipient behaves toward things neither subjectively nor objectively—indeed, he does not 'behave' at all. When perceiving, he feels as though the things were perceiving themselves, as though they were making use of his senses in order to attain the maximum fullness of being.

All this is far from being vague and nebulous. It may be so for the European, who cannot produce this state in himself without the preliminary exercises, and thus cannot appreciate the fact that this mode of immediate awareness is absolutely clear and definite. So much so, indeed, that compared with it a perception which divides itself into consciousness of the percipient and of an object must appear defective, derivative, and distorted.

Anyone who is able to experience, and be experienced, in this way argues more from the standpoint of things than of himself. He allows each thing to attain its full existence, as though it had a right to it. The Zen Buddhist can do this because his experience has given him a respect for everything that is, just as it is, including all living things. He meets it with a non-imposing of his own will, but at the same time he does not let himself be influenced by *its* will. He respects it as though it were a manifestation of that which underlies it, by which it is sustained. Everything that is, is embraced and sustained by the One—God, Nothing, All. Thus far he could subscribe to the formula of pantheism.

All this seems so clear and simple—and yet how much contradicts it, above all in relation to the human world (indeed, *only* in relation to this world). If it were not in a bad way, what need would there be of Zen? What need of this rigorous work on oneself to establish contact with the heart of being?

But it is equally undeniable that, as the mystical experience runs its course, it takes on more and more clearly the following structure: Nothing takes the place of Being, and, just as unexpectedly, Being takes the place of Nothing.

Until one day, as the culmination of this experience, in which you are changed from something into nothing and from nothing into something, illumination comes: The Void is just exactly All. It is the very being of Being—and it is not; it is just simply Nothing—and it is not.

It is this thing here—and it is not; and this thing here is itself, and again it is not. In short, every single thing is the exponent of Nothing—and it is not.

Then that is the truth—so simple? So simple that compared with it the pantheistic interpretation— false though it be—seems complicated.

So it is for this that one has laboured a life long —to stumble on something so simple! Yes, but one must add at once: this truth is a real, palpable thing. There is no doubt about its absolute certainty. You *see* it in a seeing that is not-seeing, a knowing that is not-knowing.

Anyone who has had this experience of illumination (in which Nothing illumines itself) will no longer even understand the meaning of questions asked out of theoretical curiosity: Why is Nothing the essence of Being, how does Nothing become Something? How Something becomes Nothing— one knows that from practical experience. Hence the Zen Buddhist's rejection of all such specula- tions. The more uncomplicated the experience is, the better. So here too: let it be what it is, and not think that something must be added.

The Zen Buddhist is open to all and everything, without reserve—he has no dogmatic allegiances —and so also to science. Nor does he reject rationality as such, only its claim to play a role in mysticism.

Even in the simplest conditions he lives an im- mensely rich spiritual life. He cannot do other- wise. For he no longer lives 'his' life: he *is* life to its uttermost possibility—precisely by not being it himself. Every moment for him is worth an eter- nity. He lives wholly in the present, in the here and now. Not in yesterday, not in tomorrow, and yet in them too, since they are the framework of human existence, of the flux of time.

ENLIGHTENMENT, REBIRTH, BUDDHA NATURE

Enlightenment comes precipitately and has the effect of a spiritual catastrophe—on that, all the enlightened are unanimously agreed. Your confidence in yourself, your reasoning powers, your conscience and your virtues, your convictions, standards, and values by which you once regulated your life, are suddenly of no more use. They are not tentatively set aside, subject to recall, as it were, but are extinguished as though they had never been. So irresistible is the transformative power of enlightenment that your life seems to be shifted into a new dimension, opened to new and unsuspected possibilities.

With this rebirth the enlightened at once become aware of what they are in the ground of their being: they perceive their Buddha nature. Yet it would be contrary to the facts of experience to call this nature the 'better self' or 'real ego', or even the 'super-ego'. In this 'primary sphere'[1] there is nothing like an ego or self any more. This original nature is, rather, the selfless and egoless Ground, the nameless and formless root of the self.

Asked what the Buddha nature is, the Zen Buddhist would probably answer: 'It is unmoved.' But if an attempt were made to hold him to this, pointing out the dialectical difficulties of relationship between this unmoved ground of the soul and

[1] Herrigel was already interested in elaborating the idea of the 'primary sphere' in his first major philosophical work, *Urstoff und Urform*. [H.T.]

the soul's inner motion, he would wave all this talk away with a flick of his hand and declare that neither 'moved' nor 'unmoved' can be predicated of the Buddha nature. It is neither the one nor the other, it is both at once and is not. What it is can only be experienced and apprehended, but not comprehended and explained in concepts.

COMMUNICATION WITH THE WHOLE OF BEING

People are often tempted to regard the Zen Buddhist as lacking in feeling; they might even call him unfeeling—not because the deepest part of him is unmoved, for this unmovedness can no more be perceived from the outside than the surface of the sea reveals the calm of its depths. The reason is, rather, that the Zen Buddhist is wary of making a show of his feelings and dislikes clothing them in words.

Behind this dislike of words several motives lie hidden. First, his consciously cultivated, and in the end instinctive, aversion to the dishonesty of exaggerating. Because of his training, the Zen Buddhist is aware of the danger inherent in the expression of feeling: of saying more than you feel, and of meaning less than you say. He is much too sensitive to others not to realize how easy it is to rid yourself of oppressive feelings by giving expression to them. Once you have told a person who has experienced a great sorrow how deeply you commiserate with his fate, so that he feels understood and is comforted by these sympathetic words, it is only too easy to think you have done justice to him and his feelings merely by this utterance. You then lose sight of him, thinking of him only from a distance and feeling for him only in memory, and turn again undisturbed to your own affairs. In this way you destroy the true sense of feeling and become more and more superficial. But the ultimate reason—and the decisive one—is that the Zen Buddhist is far from limiting his feelings of joy and compassion to human beings and to every aspect of human existence. He embraces in these feelings everything that lives and breathes, including animals and plants, and he does not shut out even the least among them. Words are powerless here.

The fact that words act as bridges between human beings should, therefore, not beguile us into neglecting and despising those realms of existence in which words do not unite, do not establish any contact but, on the contrary, open out an abyss—as if anything that had not reached the human level had only a provisional existence and were of no importance.

Thus feelings lose nothing by not being expressed. Perhaps they even gain in sincerity and intensity the less they are verbalized. The Zen Buddhist is constantly confirmed in his experience that there is a fundamental communication which embraces all forms of existence and which, because of its immediacy, must abandon the medium of words.

For the Zen Buddhist it is a simple fact of experience that sincere feelings overleap all barriers put up by the mind. For him shared joy and shared sufferings are not feelings restricted to the private sphere—feelings that may do him credit and testify to his spiritual level, but nevertheless remain without effect and vanish as though they had never been. Rather, constantly repeated and irrefutable evidence shows that their mere existence changes the face of the world. The Zen Buddhist is therefore content to have feelings and to foster them. He does not turn them inward for his own gratification but, completely unconcerned about their fate and with no ulterior motive, allows them release in his outward behaviour. He does not pass by the joys and sufferings of others without taking them to himself and reinforcing them with his own feelings—which are yet not his own—so that their full potentialities may unfold.

Through this selfless encounter the Zen Buddhist becomes aware that life goes well for him only if he succeeds in establishing the right relationship with himself. He discovers that to be happy is not a matter of chance, but is an art than can be learned and raised to ever higher levels of intensity. To lead his life aright it is therefore necessary that he should have a revelation of what 'he himself' in truth is; that he should learn to encounter not only the world around him, but himself as well, self-lessly; to see without distortion not only the nature of the existent which he is not, but also the nature of the existent which is himself.

To the extent that he understands this, he will inquire into the 'essence' of the existent, into the all-embracing truth by virtue of which all existents *are* and he himself *is*.

By what ways he seeks to obtain an answer cannot be discussed here. Only this much can be said: that with the answer—if any answer is granted at all—comes the unequivocal experience that no efforts of interpretation, no matter how unremittingly and conscientiously pursued, lead to recognition of the truth, to ultimate knowledge.

Grasping the truth means neither more nor less than being gripped by it on a plane beyond your own thinking. For this empirical fact the Zen Buddhist has coined the term *satori*, by which he means the fundamental experience of being suddenly and violently seized upon by the truth. Indescribable in origin, underivable in content, it operates irresistibly, and no well-established habit and no reflection, however penetrating, prevails against it. The sentient ego, in an inexplicable way, becomes transparent to those states of being which are constellated by *satori* and shine in their own light.

The scope of the inner transformation that produces this transparency can hardly be estimated. Since the old, perverse consciousness of self has fallen away from the transformed personality, he no longer succumbs to the delusion that he must first *seek* contact with other human beings outside his own circle, as though the range of his human relationships depended on himself, on his good will, on his own choice. Enlightenment has made him aware that in a mysterious way and without his doing, he is originally connected with all the people in the world and with all living things, so that every relationship sought or suffered is only the revelation of this primary one.

THE ART OF COMPASSION

How enlightenment, if granted to the adept, works out in his encounter with the world and

99

with himself has already been discussed. But how does he act as a helper to others? By shared joy and suffering, it was said.

Genuine selfless joy is an art which hardly anyone understands. More difficult still is the art of suffering. Even those who have gone through much suffering are in danger of missing the right way. For the meaning of suffering is hidden, and is revealed only to him who knows how to accept and bear it. The Zen priest helps the sufferer to endure his suffering in the right way.

When a Zen priest who has taken a sufferer under his care has reason to fear that he is not equal to his suffering, he will visit him repeatedly. Not with the intention of relieving him of distracting worries, but of reaching his inner self. He will try to make him face his suffering by bringing its full extent and magnitude to consciousness. He will help the sufferer to see that great suffering is not overcome by refusing to face it or by surrendering to it in despair. He will warn him of the danger of allowing himself to be solaced, and of waiting for time to heal. Salvation lies in giving full assent to his fate, serenely accepting what is laid upon him without asking why he should be singled out for so much suffering. Whoever is able to bear suffering in this way grows to the stature of his suffering, and he detaches himself from it by learning more and more to disregard the fact that it is *his* suffering.

This detachment paves the way to healing, and healing follows of itself, the more sensitive he becomes to the suffering of others, and the more selflessly he shares their sufferings. This fellow suffering is quite different from the sentimental sympathy most of us indulge in, which, easily aroused and quickly dissipated, remains ineffective because it is not selfless enough. True compassion not bound to words forges the most intimate bond between human beings and all living creatures. The real meaning of suffering discloses itself only to him who has learned the art of compassion.

If the sufferer's ears and eyes are opened by this clarification of his state of mind, he will mark that neither flight from reality nor denial of suffering can bring him detachment. And if, thrown back on himself, he shows that he is trying to become one with his fate, to assent to it so that it can fulfil its own law, then the priest will go on helping him. He will answer his questions, without offering anything more than suggestions and, of course, without preaching.

For there is something that seems to him very much more important than words. Gradually he will fall silent, and in the end will sit there wordless, for a long time, sunk deep in himself. And the strange thing is that this silence is not felt by the other person as indifference, as a desolate emptiness which disturbs rather than calms. It is as if this silence had more meaning than countless words could ever have. It is as if he were being drawn into a field of force from which fresh strength flows into him. He feels suffused with a strange confidence, even when his visitor has long since departed. And it may be that in these joyful hours, the resolve will be born to set out on the path that turns a wretched existence into a life of happiness.